Dune Shacks

Paintings by David Forest Thompson

Dune Shacks

copyright © 2006 by David Forest Thompson

Signature Book Printing, Inc.
www.sbpbooks.com
Printed in Hong Kong

ISBN 978-0-9795511-0-9

Printed 2011
Second Edition

For more information please contact
www.davidthompsonart.com

Acknowledgements

My thanks to Deb Chmielewsky for introducing me to the dunes; Peter Clemons and Marianne Benson for letting me be a part of their family; also to Buddy, for putting up with my obsession. Many thanks to Brenda Pizzo and Kevin Tringale, Dana Faris, Richard Stimpson, Ejay Khan at Khan Studio for her artistic input, and writer, Lolli Fleming; also Janet, Connie and David Armstrong for making me feel like part of their family from the moment we met. To Levent for her love and support, and to Ray Carpenter for believing in my work and encouraging me to do more.

Introduction

At the tip of Cape Cod, Massachusetts, along a three-mile stretch of beach, there lies a world unto itself. Hidden along this ever-changing coastline are a number of dwellings appropriately called "Dune Shacks". These shacks have all - in some way - changed lives, inspired, educated, comforted, and awed. Everyone I have ever spoken with that has had an experience out here had a story to tell. This is my story.

On a Sunday afternoon nearly ten years ago, an impromptu visit to friends staying in one of the Provincetown dune shacks changed me forever. I couldn't have imagined how a group of simple and primitive cottages with no electricity or running water, weathered from years of battling the Atlantic Ocean at their doorstep could resonate so powerfully for me. Dotting the landscape of the outer Cape's backshore, these structures are much more than shelter from the ocean beyond. The harsh beauty of these dwellings drew me in immediately and what began as an appreciation of the simple, unaffected structures has evolved into an artist's love affair. Over the next three summers I painted each of the 18 shacks, telling their stories with color and texture. Each painting has been a labor of love.

I am drawn, powerfully and mostly inexplicably, to the solitude and simplicity of life on the dunes. The dunes and their dwellings have been a muse of sorts, and I've become their student. I've learned that each structure has its own history; each its own mystique. Some have housed artists and writers. Others have been shared across generations, a crucial and beloved piece of a family's bond. All are rich in memories and stories, a haven from the rush of life beyond this spectacular place.

For those who will listen, each has its own story. Central to each of the shacks is how they came to be, and whether the beauty, solitude and inspiration will be a part of their future. A life saving station at nearby Peaked Hill Bars was in operation into the 1920s, accounting for the Guards' presence there. Some of the shacks were built by them.

Many creative individuals spent time in the shacks. Playwright Eugene O'Neil, Agnus Bolton, Jack Kerouac, Boris Margo, Jan Gelb, poet Harry Kemp, Hazel Hawthorne Werner and many more.

The Cape Cod National Seashore was formed in the 1960s, encompassing the shoreline shacks. While one cottage is privately owned, all 18 shacks have withstood the effects of nature and man trials for over a half century. Wind, snow, flooding, erosion - both elemental and manmade, efforts to protect and to secure the dunes themselves have left their touch on each cottage.

I hope you'll enjoy the paintings throughout this book and that perhaps it will spark a memory for you or lure you into the magic of the shacks. Perhaps it will entice you to learn more or even to visit the dune shacks yourself.

In this ever-changing landscape, what we see one day might not be there the next.

David Forest Thompson

This cottage was owned at one time by artist, Jean Cohen, and her husband, John Grille, also a painter. The Cohen shack was, and still is, a popular shack for artists. Jan Muller, Marcia Marcus and many others painted here.

The daily ritual, filling the shower bag and hanging it in the hot sun, so later that day I would be able to rinse the salt from my skin.

5. *Fleurant Shack*
Oil on canvas, 16" x 20"

6. *Fleurant*
Oil on board, 8" x 10"

The Fleurant Shack - known to everyone who visited the dunes.
Leo Fleurant lived on the dunes for thirty some years.

7. *Adams Guest Cottage*
Oil on board, 11" x 14"

8. *David Adams Shack*
Oil on canvas, 20" x 24"

"Coming out here for the first time changed my life, the way I look at everything. I realized you could live without things; that this was enough."

The clouds were moving so fast,
the grass was blowing wildly,
crisp cold air. It was very busy, yet nothing was happening.

9. *Mission Bell in Winter*
Oil on board, 20" x 24"

10. *Mission Bell*
Oil on canvas, 28" x 32"

The Champlin's have lived on the dunes for 30 some years. Nate Champlin's collection of rare bottles can be seen at the Provincetown Heritage Museum.

"**A**t night there are a million stars. It's incredible, truly a way of living that should be preserved."

Conrad Malicoat's Shack was built in the early 50's, then rebuilt in 1959 or 1960.
This is one of my favorite views.

12. *Euphoria in Fog*
Acrylic on canvas, 20" x 24"

13. *Euphoria Shack*
Oil on board, 12"x16"

Euphoria in a fog; so low you can walk through it and feel it, but you can't touch it.

Hazel Hawthorne had two cottages, "Thalassa" and "Euphoria". Author of a novel about Provincetown entitled "The Salt Box", she entertained the likes of Norman Mailer, Edmond Leighton, Curt Valentine and others.

"I feel like I've always been here, like it's a part of me. There's so much going on our here. It has become a way of life. The paintings are my way of sharing it with the world." DFT

14. *Side of Tasha*
Oil on board, 8"x10"

15. *Tasha Shack*
Oil on board, 8"x10"

Permanent Collection, Pilgrim Monument and Provincetown Museum

16. Backshore
Oil on board, 8"x10"

17. Tasha Shack II
Oil on board, 16"x20"

18. *Fowler Table*
Acrylic on canvas, 16" x 20"

19. *Fowler Interior*
Acrylic on canvas, 28" x 36"

This table is where I sat and painted many of my works. I can still feel the warm summer breeze blowing through the shack when I look at this painting.

20. *Fowler Shack*
Oil on board, 5" x 7"

21. **Dune Shack Kitchen**
Acrylic on canvas, 28" x 36"

22. *Fowler in Winter*
Acrylic on canvas, 11" x 14"

February - no sign of life out here this time of year, you are truly alone.

This gnarly tree caught my eye as it stood guard over Zara.

24. *The Grail II*
Oil on board, 8"x10"

25. *The Grail*
Acrylic on canvas, 36"x36"

26. *Lightning on the Dunes*
Oil on canvas, 20"x24"

The Grail is wet from a summer rain, all the colors are intensified.
The shingles on the shack are a dark charcoal gray, unlike the typical sun bleached gray.
The color of the sky, so intense, and that lightning bolt!

27. *Grail from top of Dune*
Oil on canvas, 11" x 14"

"It took me three summers to paint them all. The way of life out here is different. There's no electricity, you pump your own water. I wanted people to see the way of life experienced out here." DFT

Dune dwellers, Marianne Benson and Peter Clemons

"It's really documenting history. I wanted people to see this world as I saw it . . .
After that first day, it was in my blood and I knew I had to paint them all." DFT

29. *Frenchie's Late Summer*
Oil on board, 16" x 20"

30. *Frenchie Shack*
Oil on linen, 9" x 14"

Jeannie "Frenchie" Chanel, a chorus girl from George White's "Scandels", came to town with Bette Davis. Davis left, but Frenchie fell in love with the Cape and stayed.

The only clothes dryer out here is a line between two posts.
Everything about the way of life here is simplicity.

That Sunday started my love affair with the dunes. The perfect summer day: the sun, the sand, the food and drink, and all the people I love.

Thalassa at sunrise. I decided the first thing I saw that morning was worthy of painting. But then, everything I see I tend to view as art.

34. *Full Moon at the Outhouse*
Acrylic on canvas, 11" x 14"

35. *Thalassa Interior*
Oil on canvas, 28" x 32"

Debbie at her command post. The best place to see what's going on (which was usually us) and on and on.

Built in 1931, this cottage has the only year round resident.

"I come here even in the winter. I pack a lunch, walk over the dunes, go inside, turn on the gas stove and make a cup of hot chocolate. It's great think time." DFT

40. *Charlie Schmid*
Oil on canvas, 16" x 20"

The tearing down of Charlie's Shack started the struggle to save the rest from the same fate.

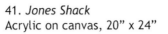
41. *Jones Shack*
Acrylic on canvas, 20" x 24"

The Jones Shack sits high on a dune, far away from the others. The perfect retreat

Since 1936, the same family has summered in this shack.

There is nothing like a full moon in the dunes, accompanied by a royal blue sky.

When was the last time you were in total solitude? All you hear in these dunes is the wind and the ocean. It's an experience that changes the way you look at life.

The light here is like no other.

This little red enamel teapot, I was told, has lived in Thalassa Shack on a rusty nail over the stove for many years.

List of Paintings

Cover Painting: *Seaside Cottage*, Oil on canvas, 16" x 20"
Inside Cover Photograph: *Mother Dune*
Title Page: *Cottage on Backshore*, Oil on canvas, 24"x32"

1. *C-Scape*, Oil on board, 16" x 20"
2. *On the Way to the Shack*, Oil on canvas, 20" x 24"
3. *Outdoor Shower*, Oil on canvas, 16" x 20"
4. *Return from the Beach*, Oil on canvas, 24" x 36"
5. *Fleurant Shack*, Oil on canvas, 16" x 20"
6. *Fleurant*, Oil on board, 8" x 10"
7. *Adams Guest Cottage*, Oil on board, 11" x 14"
8. *David Adams Shack*, Oil on canvas, 20" x 24"
9. *Mission Bell in Winter*, Oil on board, 20" x 24"
10. *Mission Bell*, Oil on canvas, 28" x 32"
11. *Malicoat*, Acrylic on canvas, 20" x 24"
12. *Euphoria in Fog*, Acrylic on canvas, 20" x 24"
13. *Euphoria Shack*, Oil on board, 12" x 16"
14. *Side of Tasha*, Oil on board, 8" x 10"
15. *Tasha Shack*, Oil on board, 8" x 10"
16. *Backshore*, Oil on board, 8" x 10"
17. Harry Kemp Shack (*Tasha Shack*), Oil on board, 16" x 20"
18. *Fowler Table*, Acrylic on canvas, 16" x 20"
19. *Fowler Interior*, Acrylic on canvas, 28" x 36"
20. *Fowler Shack*, Oil on board, 5" x 7"
21. *Dune Shack Kitchen*, Acrylic on canvas, 28" x 36"
22. *Fowler in Winter*, Acrylic on canvas, 11" x 14"
23. *Zara*, Oil on canvas, 16" x 20"
24. *The Grail II*, Oil on board, 8" x 10"
25. *The Grail*, Acrylic on canvas, 36" x 36"
26. *Lightning on the Dunes*, Oil on canvas, 20" x 24"
27. *Grail from Top of Dune*, Oil on canvas, 11" x 14"
28. *The Grail Late Afternoon*, Oil on board, 16" x 20"
29. *Frenchie's Late Summer*, Oil on board, 16" x 20"
30. *Frenchie Shack*, Oil on linen, 9" x 14"
31. *Frenchie's Shack*, Photograph
32. *Sunday with Friends*, Acrylic on canvas, 16" x 20"
33. *Thalassa at Sunrise*, Acrylic on canvas, 20" x 24"
34. *Full Moon at the Outhouse*, Acrylic on canvas, 11" x 14"
35. *Thalassa Interior*, Oil on canvas, 28" x 32"
36. *Deb on Ladder*, Acrylic on board, 16" x 20"
37. *Beach Cottage*, Oil on canvas, 8" x 10"
38. *Peg's in Winter*, Acrylic on canvas, 8" x 10"
39. *Peg Watson Interior*, Oil on board, 11" x 14"
40. *Charlie Schmid*, Oil on canvas, 16" x 20"
41. *Jones Shack*, Acrylic on canvas, 20" x 24"
42. *Ray Well's Shack*, Acrylic on canvas, 20" x 24"
43. *Armstrong Shack*, Oil on canvas, 11" x 14"
44. *C-Scape at Dawn*, Oil on board, 8" x 10"
45. *Hazel's Teapot*, Oil on board, 8" x 10"

Back Cover Painting, *Pink Sky*, Oil on canvas, 16" x 20"

David Forest Thompson

Born in England in 1958, David grew up as an Air Force brat living in Kansas, Wyoming, Texas and California, before settling in the Boston area. He is self-taught, working mostly with oil on canvas or board. David is also a photographer, and has this to say about his photographs: "Every time I take a photograph, I see it as a potential painting. Some of these photos may very well end up on canvas."

In 1988 David opened Eclipse Salon Gallery, the first hair salon/art gallery on Newbury Street, allowing him to combine both of his talents. He not only enjoys painting just on the dunes or on the cape but throughout New England and where ever his travels take him throughout the world. David resides in Dorchester, MA with his partner.

David may be the only person to have painted all the shacks. He won't assert that for a fact, but he has not been able to find anyone else who has. It started when a serendipitous walk into the dunes introduced him to the removed world of the dune shacks.

www.davidthompsonart.com